The Fruit & Berry Smoothie Recipe Book

Quick & Easy Smoothies for Your Enjoyment and Healthy Eating Every Day

Amanda Green

CONTENTS

CONTENTS	**2**
FRUIT & BERRY SMOOTHIES	**6**
HELPFUL TIPS FOR MAKING SMOOTHIES	**10**
RULES FOR CONSUMING SMOOTHIES	**12**
BERRY SMOOTHIES	**14**
Strawberry Breeze	18
Creamy Strawberries	20
Strawberries, Raspberry & Lime	22
Strawberries & Basil	24
Strawberry, Banana & Oatmeal	26
Sparkling Strawberry	28
Berry Mix & Oat Flakes	30
Chocolate Strawberries & Raspberry	32
Blackberries & Red Currants	34
Red & Black Currant	36
Blackcurrant & Pineapple	38
Currants, Strawberries & Raspberries	40
Blueberries with Pear	42
Blueberries & Banana	44
Blueberries & Oatmeal	46
Cranberry & Oatmeal	48
Cranberry & Apple	50
Ginger Cranberry	52
Cranberries & Raspberries	54
Cranberries & Ginger	56

PEACH & APRICOT SMOOTHIES   **58**

    PEACH & BANANA   62
    PEACHES & CHERRIES   64
    ICE PEACH   66
    APRICOT & PEACH   68
    APRICOT & STRAWBERRY   70
    APRICOTS & ORANGE   72
    APRICOT & BANANA   74

APPLE & PEAR SMOOTHIES   **76**

    APPLE, PEAR & BASIL   80
    APPLE & BANANA   82
    APPLE & MANGO   84
    SAVORY APPLE & PEAR   86
    APPLE, BANANA & OATMEAL   88
    APPLES & SPICES   90
    APPLE & LEMON   92
    PEAR & GINGER   94
    MINT PEAR   96
    PEAR & SPICES   98

CHERRY & SWEET CHERRY SMOOTHIES   **100**

    SWEET CHERRY & OATMEAL   104
    CHERRIES & SPICE   106
    SWEET CHERRIES & STRAWBERRIES   108
    CHERRIES & CHOCOLATE   110
    CHERRY, APPLE & BANANA   112
    PIQUANT CHERRY WITH BASIL   114
    CHERRIES, BANANA & COCONUT   116
    GINGER CHERRY   118

TROPICAL FRUIT SMOOTHIE   **120**

    KIWI & MANGO   124
    CREAMY KIWI   126

KIWI, BANANA & CHIA SEEDS	128
KIWI & NECTARINE	130
MANGO SURPRISE	132
MANGO, APPLE & BASIL	134
MANGO & BANANA	136
PINEAPPLE DELIGHT	138
PINEAPPLE & COCONUT	140
PINEAPPLE & APPLE	142
HEAVENLY COCONUT DELIGHT	144
PAPAYA, ORANGE & PINEAPPLE	146
PAPAYA & BANANA	148
VANILLA PAPAYA	150

CITRUS SMOOTHIES — **152**

MINT ORANGE	156
ORANGE & GINGER	158
SPICY ORANGE	160
ORANGE & MANGO	162
LEMON, COCONUT & GINGER	164
INVIGORATING GRAPEFRUIT & CITRUS	166
GRAPEFRUIT & STRAWBERRIES	168
GRAPEFRUIT & BANANA	170
GRAPEFRUIT & PINEAPPLE	172

MELON & WATERMELON SMOOTHIE — **174**

MELON, MINT & LEMON	178
MELON & BANANA	180
MELON & KIWI	182
MELON & BERRIES	184
WATERMELON & GRAPEFRUIT	186
WATERMELON & BANANA	188
WATERMELON "MOJITO"	190
WATERMELON, MELON & RASPBERRY	192
WATERMELON & STRAWBERRIES	194
WATERMELON & BLACKCURRANT	196

INDEX 198

Fruit & Berry Smoothies

Bananas, strawberries, berries, and other fruits: the thought of these smoothies makes your head dizzy. With a handful of berries, fruit, natural yogurt, and juice on hand, you can recharge your energy every morning with these delicious, healthy, and nutritious smoothies that are made in minutes. This delicacy is even healthier than freshly squeezed juice. And, a smoothie made from frozen fruit can be used as a substitute for ice cream. But unlike traditional ice cream, it is healthier and more nutritious. The perfect substitute for unhealthy desserts!

Fruit smoothies are of great benefit to the body for many reasons. As you know, fruit is an excellent source of vitamins, minerals, and a host of other health benefits. Fruit also provides us with a large amount of dietary fiber, thanks to which our intestines are cleansed of toxins. Fiber also helps us stay full longer, and lowers cholesterol and blood sugar.

The lack of heat treatment of smoothies allows you to keep almost all the elements in their original form. It is much easier for the body to assimilate the beneficial components from raw foods. But it is important to remember that in the presence of chronic gastrointestinal tract diseases, some raw fruits, even chopped, can provoke an exacerbation.

So, if you feel heavy in your body, and lack sleep and energy, try drinking a glass of vitamin smoothie instead of coffee in the morning after waking up.

Benefits of fruit smoothies:

The addition of banana - supports the work of the heart muscle and restores the salt balance in the body due to the high content of potassium;

Strawberries significantly accelerate metabolic processes, which, as you know, is the key to tangible weight loss. Strawberry smoothies can help deal with internal tissue damage;

Blueberries have always been associated with a natural regulator of vision quality for many people, but modern research has shown that this tiny berry also helps with weight loss;

An apple smoothie is an excellent treatment for and prevention of iron deficiency anemia since ripe fruits are rich in iron;

Pears profitably "deceive" the body with their chemical composition, and a person stays full longer than usual;

Kiwi in cocktails will help improve immunity, as it contains a lot of ascorbic acids; kiwi is also very rich in insoluble fiber, which surprisingly improves the digestive process.

Pomegranate reduces appetite well, removes harmful substances from the body, and also helps prevent certain diseases, for example, atherosclerosis;

Mango increases libido and mood, promoting the release of oxytocin and endorphins;

Orange pulp and lemon juice in a smoothie will help fight autumn blues and depression, and a high content of vitamin C helps prevent colds;

Pineapple in a smoothie is the perfect solution for losing weight.

Coconut or coconut milk are great substitutes for the sweets you crave when dieting. Forget the cakes, add some coconut to your smoothie and enjoy the sweetest drink that won't hurt your figure.

The best fruit smoothie recipes are usually quite simple, but very healthy and delicious. In this book, you will find a collection of our best fruit smoothie recipes.

Whatever ingredients you currently have on hand, such as bananas, apples, oranges, pears, citrus fruits, or exotic fruits, we will most likely have a recipe for you!

Helpful Tips for Making Smoothies

At first glance, making a smoothie is easy.

But even such an easy-to-prepare drink has its own rules, forgetting about which, you can get a completely different result than you expected.

What needs to be considered so that your drink is not only healthy but also as tasty as possible? We share useful tips.

Multiple tastes can spoil the drink. Anything with more than 5 ingredients in a smoothie can spoil the taste. The drink comes out incomprehensibly, with a vague smell and indistinct taste.

If you are allergic to certain types of fruit or milk, exclude them from the formula or easily replace them with other ingredients.

Thoroughly rinse the berries and fruit before adding them to the blender, because they won't be heated.

Try not to add sugar, ice cream, or cream to the drink if you are watching your figure.

Do not add only sweet or too thick fruits to smoothies, keep balance and experiment: this way you will find your perfect recipe and you can even delight yourself with your favorite smoothies every day.

Watch the color of the products. Mixing green with red will give an unappetizing muddy brown. This smoothie is not pleasing to the eye.

The drink should be creamy. This requires a powerful blender. And nuts, fruits, and greens must be chopped until smooth, mashed potatoes.

Add water or other liquid components little by little. If you overdo it, you get a faded compote with floating fruit particles.

Rules for Consuming Smoothies

How Often Can I Drink Smoothies?

There are no rules about the number of smoothies you can or cannot drink each day. Likewise, there are no regulations about the size you should consume. You can read different recommendations in different sources. Someone writes that 1-2 glasses of cocktail (250-500 ml) per day will be enough. Someone recommends drinking 1 liter or more smoothies per day. There are many studies and conflicting opinions. The best solution is to try various options and determine what works best for you.

However, you should not get carried away with smoothies so

as to replace all meals with them, especially if you go on a strict diet in the form of smoothies.

This can have an undesirable effect on the functioning of the gastrointestinal tract. For the intestines to function properly, solid food is needed every day as talked about in the previous chapter.

When Should You Drink a Smoothie During the Day?

Smoothies are most commonly taken as a snack. Plus, a smoothie is an acceptable and reliable breakfast. Sometimes when you're struggling with insomnia, a smoothie can be a great dinner.

Fruit smoothies contain quite a lot of fructose, so it is better to drink them in the morning in order to have time to use up all the energy received from the drink. Green and vegetable smoothies are ideal for an afternoon snack or light dinner.

Buy or Make?

Thick cocktails are offered by many cafes and restaurants; ready-made versions are sold in supermarkets. However, the most delicious and healthy smoothie will be the one you make with your own hands!

Nutritionists around the world claim that it is best to make a smoothie at home. The reason is simple: you know exactly what products go into the finished shake. This, in turn, allows you to change the composition at your discretion, as well as personally control the amount of sugar. The thing is that for a smoothie, the sweetness that fruits and berries give is enough, however, various sweeteners and preservatives are additionally added to store cocktails.

Berry Smoothies

The benefits of berries have long been known. Berries are no longer a seasonal delicacy and can now be eaten all year round.

The benefits of berries are undeniable for our health. In addition to vitamins and trace elements, berries contain fiber, which is necessary for the intestines, and antioxidants, which can stop the aging process.

Berry smoothies are real antioxidant bombs for our bodies. Moreover, the brighter the berries, the more antioxidants they contain.

If you want to live a long life and not get sick, be sure to eat more fresh berries, which are also useful in the fact that they help in the prevention of colds and infectious diseases, treat arthritis, normalize blood pressure, and reduce risk of memory loss in old age.

Currant

Of all types of currants, black currants are the most useful, they contain the most macro-and micro-elements and are rich in vitamins C, P, and K. Currants are useful for stomach ulcers, gastritis with low acidity of gastric contents, atherosclerosis, kidney disease, metabolic disorders ... During the period of viral diseases, it is useful to use black currant to increase immunity.

Red currant berries increase appetite and quickly quench thirst, they are used as an antipyretic and mild laxative.

Raspberries

Fragrant raspberries will decorate any dessert or smoothie, and in itself – they are a storehouse of vitamins. The berries contain vitamins C, B1, B12, PP, copper, iron, potassium, fiber, pectins. Raspberries contain salicylic acid, which has a pronounced antipyretic effect. Thanks to the action of phytoncides, raspberries destroy the spores of fungi and staphylococci.

Raspberries also have a diaphoretic effect that can help reduce heat.

Strawberry

The beneficial properties of strawberries and wild strawberries will help in the prevention and treatment of vision problems. Red berries contain vitamins of group B, C, carotene, folic acid, fiber, pectins, organic acids, iron, iodine, potassium, phosphorus, calcium, manganese.

Blueberry

This berry is considered one of the very first in terms of its usefulness for our health. Blueberries are rich in substances essential for the full-fledged life of a person - lactic, citric, cinchona, oxalic, and other acids, as well as microelements. Like all berries, blueberries are on the list of recommended foods when dieting. In addition, blueberries contain antioxidants, the use of berries helps to maintain visual acuity, strengthens the cardiovascular system, and helps to resist infectious diseases.

Blackberries

Blackberries are a good source of folate, B vitamins, which help keep hair healthy, reduce the risk of cardiovascular disease, and improve mood. The antioxidants in blackberries help with arthritis, age-related memory loss, cataracts, and other vision problems. Also, the use of this healthy berry will help lower blood cholesterol levels, and this berry is also important for anyone diagnosed with type 2 diabetes.

The benefits of a berry smoothie will be maximized if you take into account simple rules during the preparation process.

You should choose seedless berries. These are raspberries, strawberries, blackberries, watermelon pulp. Cherries and sweet cherries can be used after the seeds have been extracted.

Before preparing the drink, you should carefully sort out all the berries, rinse and dry. If you start chopping wet fruit right after washing, the smoothie will turn out to be too watery; even if at first glance the berries look almost dry, they still have a lot of moisture.

Strawberry smoothies are the easiest to make and provide the most benefits and flavor. Ideal combinations are with banana, mango, nectarine, watermelon, or peach. Strawberry and melon smoothies will delight even the most sophisticated gourmet.

You can use vanilla, cinnamon, ginger as a seasoning for berry smoothies. Sweet lovers can add honey, maple syrup, agave syrup, and other sweeteners. But people looking to lose weight are better off using zero-calorie sweeteners.

How to use frozen berries

Fresh berries are only available for a couple of months a year, so frozen berries are used much more often than fresh ones.

Does freezing spoil the taste of berries?

Freezing mainly affects appearance: ice breaks the internal structure of the berry, it becomes flabby, watery. The taste of frozen berries remains virtually unchanged.

To defrost or not?

For smoothies, it is better to half defrost the berries – otherwise, you risk breaking the blender blades.

If defrosting, six hours before using, transfer the bag or container of berries from the freezer to the refrigerator compartment. The slower the fruits are thawed, the less likely they are to turn into porridge. A faster way is to put the sealed bag of berries in a large container of cold water - this will reduce the defrosting time to an hour and a half.

Strawberry Breeze

A bright, refreshing, low-calorie smoothie with an incredible strawberry flavor and aroma.

Strawberry not only has a magical taste and delicious aroma, it improves digestion, improves immunity, normalizes salt metabolism in the body, and also slows down the aging process.

Ingredients

1 cup fresh strawberries
1 banana
1 apple
2 sprigs of mint
1 tbsp. l. lime juice
1/2 glass of mineral water (still)
1 pinch of vanilla
Sweetener (optional)
Coconut flakes (for decoration)
Ice cubes

Instructions

Remove the leaves from the strawberries, rinse well.

Peel the apple, remove the core. Peel the banana. Cut the prepared fruit into pieces.

Detach the fresh mint leaves from the twigs, rinse with water and dry a little with a paper towel.

Pour the mineral water into a blender bowl, add the strawberries and mint leaves, beat until smooth.

Then add slices of apple and banana, sprinkle with vanilla. Squeeze the juice out of the lime and add to the smoothie. Whisk again along with the fruit and toppings.

For sweetness, you can use any natural sweetener, such as honey or agave syrup.

Pour the finished smoothie into glasses, place a few small strawberries on top, sprinkle with coconut, and garnish with fresh mint.

Creamy Strawberries

Sweet strawberries are a delicious food to start your morning routine.

Blended with sweet bananas and strawberry yogurt, this recipe delivers a nutritious, complex carbohydrate boost that will keep you energized for a long time.

Ingredients

2 cups strawberries

1 banana, peeled

1 cup of strawberry yogurt

½ cup coconut milk

¼ glass of ice

Instructions

Wash the strawberries under running cold water, sort and remove the sepals. If the strawberries are large, cut them in half.

Peel the banana, cut it into slices.

In a blender, combine the strawberries, banana, yogurt, and coconut milk with ¼ cup ice and beat until smooth.

While stirring, add the remaining ice until the desired consistency is achieved.

Strawberries, Raspberry & Lime

The tart sensation of limes gets chilled out with the sweet taste of strawberries, raspberries, and strawberry yogurt.

When there's a delicious blend like this, it's pretty easy to live a healthy and happy life!

Ingredients

1 cup strawberries

1 cup raspberries

1 lime, peeled and seeded

1 cup of strawberry yogurt

1 cup of ice

½ cup of water

Instructions

Wash the strawberries under running cold water, sort and remove the sepals.

If the strawberries are large, cut them in half. Transfer the berries to a blender.

In a blender, combine the strawberries, raspberries, lime, and yogurt with ½ cup ice and beat until smooth.

While stirring, add the water and the remaining ice until the desired consistency is achieved.

Strawberries & Basil

This is an incredibly tasty and healthy strawberry and aromatic basil smoothie.

This smoothie will help you lose weight and rejuvenate and saturate the body with vitamins and essential trace elements.

Several sprigs of basil will accentuate the strawberry flavor and add a spicy flavor to the drink.

Ingredients

2 cups fresh strawberries

2-3 sprigs of fresh basil

1 cup milk (almond or soy can be used) or yogurt

5 ice cubes

Honey or agave syrup to taste

Instructions

Wash the strawberries under running cold water, sort and remove the sepals. If the strawberries are large, cut them in half. Transfer the berries to a blender.

Wash and dry the basil. Separate the leaves from the stems. Add the basil, ice, and cold milk or yogurt to the strawberries. You can add some sweetener to your smoothie if you like.

Grind the ingredients in a blender at maximum speed until a smooth texture is obtained.

Pour the finished smoothie into transparent glasses or wine glasses, garnish with strawberries and a leaf of basil.

Strawberry, Banana & Oatmeal

A Strawberry Banana Smoothie is quick, easy, and incredibly delicious. The combination of banana and strawberry is a classic that conquered many lovers of fruit and berry flavors.

The sweetness of the banana is in perfect harmony with the light, fresh sourness of the strawberry. And this duo can be made even more useful by adding oatmeal to it.

Ideal for people in a rush in the morning. You don't have to give up a good breakfast because it can be prepared very quickly!

Ingredients

- 1 cup strawberries
- 1 banana
- 2 tablespoons instant oatmeal
- 1 cup coconut milk or yogurt
- 1 teaspoon honey (optional)

Instructions

Grind the oatmeal almost into flour.
Peel the banana, cut it into slices, and place it in a bowl of oatmeal.

Wash the strawberries and remove the sepals. Add the strawberries to a bowl. Grind the banana and strawberries with the oatmeal until it becomes a thick puree.

Pour in milk or yogurt. Add honey to taste. Stir again and let the oatmeal swell for 5-10 minutes.

Pour the strawberry banana oat smoothie into glasses and serve.

Bon Appetite!

Sparkling Strawberry

The "sparkle" of this smoothie comes from the delectable addition of ginger that makes every sip a striking one!

When there's a delicious blend like this, it's pretty easy to live a healthy and happy life!

Ingredients

- 2 cups strawberries
- 1 tablespoon grated ginger
- 1 glass of natural yogurt
- ¼ glass of ice

Instructions

Wash the strawberries under running cold water, sort and remove the sepals. If the strawberries are large, cut them in half.

In a blender, combine the strawberries, ginger, and yogurt with ¼ cup ice and beat until smooth.

While mixing, add the remaining ice until the desired consistency is achieved.

Berry Mix & Oat Flakes

The cold season is not a reason to deny yourself a colorful berry smoothie for breakfast.

After all, a delicious smoothie filled with vitamins, and the aromas and flavors of a sunny summer can be easily prepared from frozen berries.

Such a quick, healthy, and appetizing snack will give you a boost of energy, vigor, and good mood, and also pleasantly diversify your diet.

Try it!

Ingredients

1 cup frozen berry blend (any combination of strawberries, raspberries, currants, blackberries, blueberries)

1 ripe banana

2-4 tbsp instant oat flakes

1-1.5 cups apple juice

Honey - optional

Instructions

In a blender bowl, combine the frozen berries and apple juice. Whisk the mixture until smooth for a few minutes.

If you prefer the drink to be at room temperature, defrost the berries first.

Grind the oatmeal almost into flour.

Add ripe banana and 2-4 tablespoons oat flakes, and, if necessary, a little honey, or another sweetener of your choice. Whisk the mixture for a few more seconds.

You can adjust the thickness of the drink to your liking by adding more oatmeal or juice.

Chocolate Strawberries & Raspberry

Try to combine two bright summer flavors: raspberries and strawberries and remember the hot, warm days. Berries can be used both frozen and fresh.

A little grated chocolate to enhance the flavor, and unflavored yogurt for the milk base. Smoothie lovers will appreciate the freshness and rich taste of the resulting drink.

Ingredients

1 cup raspberries

1 cup strawberries

1 cup natural yogurt

2-3 squares of dark chocolate

Instructions

Sort the fresh ripe strawberries and raspberries carefully, wash in running water, remove the sepals. If you are using frozen berries, rinse in warm water.

Pour the raspberries and strawberries in the specified proportion into the blender container. Pour yogurt over everything. Rub the chocolate into fine shavings and add to the berries as well.

Turn on the blender for 60 seconds. Pour the finished raspberry smoothie into glasses. Sprinkle with the rest of the grated chocolate on top. Garnish with the most beautiful berries if desired and serve.

Blackberries & Red Currants

Blackberries are incredibly beautiful and healthy berries. Blackberries, like other berries, are a complete vitamin complex.

It is important to consume them regularly throughout the season, this will allow the body to stock up on the necessary substances and increase the state of immunity.

Ingredients

1 cup blackberries
1/3 cup red currant
1/2 banana
1/2 cup coconut milk
1 cup thick yogurt
a pinch of vanillin
2 teaspoons honey
Filling: berries, coconut; mint.

Instructions

Rinse the berries and dry a little, separate the currants from the twigs. Peel the banana, cut it and place it in the freezer for 20-30 minutes.

Combine the prepared berries, coconut milk, and banana in a blender bowl.

Add the yogurt, vanilla, and 2 teaspoons of honey.

Mix the mass at a low speed quite a bit, so that the honey dissolves in the yogurt as much as possible, but the mixture does not become very liquid.

Decorate with coconut flakes, red currant sprigs, and mint leaves.

Red & Black Currant

Red and black currants are very peculiar berries, with a pronounced sourness, but in combination with sweet fruits and yogurt, they create a drink with a delicate and pleasant taste. Currant berries are famous for the highest vitamin C content among many berries and even outstrip citrus fruits. So what could be better than starting your day with such a "vitamin bomb"?

Ingredients

1/2 cup red currant

1/2 cup black currant

1 banana

1/2 cup natural yogurt

200 g creamy ice cream

Sweetener to taste (agave syrup, honey)

Instructions

Separate the currants from the branches, rinse well and let the water drain.
Transfer the currants to a blender container and beat until thick.

Peel the banana from the top layer, cut or break into pieces and add to the other ingredients. Add ice cream, yogurt, and sweetener to taste and beat until smooth.

Pour the smoothie into glasses, garnish with berries and mint.

Blackcurrant & Pineapple

This smoothie tastes rich, similar to berry yogurt, only healthier.

This vitamin dessert is good to make to strengthen the immune system and maintain a great mood.

Try it, you will like it.

Ingredients

1 cup Blackcurrant

1/2 Pineapple

1 bunch Mint

2 cups Soy milk

Agave syrup or honey to taste

Instructions

Peel the pineapple half, core, and cut into medium pieces.

Tear off the mint leaves from the stems, set aside a few for decoration.

Put the chopped pineapple, blackcurrant, and mint leaves in a blender and fill with soy milk (you can replace it with regular milk or any other of your choice).

Stir in a blender at maximum speed for 5 minutes.

Serve garnished with mint leaves.

Tips: If you use not fresh, but frozen blackcurrant, then you can either defrost it or put it in frozen, then the smoothie will be cold, but no less tasty.

If the pineapple is not very sweet, then the smoothie may be quite sour due to the currants, so add 1 or 2 tablespoons of agave syrup or light honey to taste and punch again.

Currants, Strawberries & Raspberries

This smoothie will delight the whole family - from kids to grandparents. In hot weather, it will come in handy: it can be served for an afternoon snack or even for lunch - it is an excellent substitute for heavy meals.

The type of berries and proportions can be changed based on taste preferences (or what was found in the kitchen).

Ingredients

Currants, strawberries, raspberries - 1/3 cup each

1 cup milk or yogurt

3-4 ice cubes

1 banana and half a teaspoon of honey (optional)

mint and berries for decoration

Instructions

Sort the fresh ripe strawberries, currants, and raspberries carefully, wash in running water and remove the sepals.

If you are using frozen berries, rinse in warm water.
Mix in a blender with milk or yogurt, and add a few ice cubes.

For a sweeter and thicker smoothie, add one banana or add half a teaspoon of honey.

Pour into glasses, garnish with berries and mint and enjoy!

Blueberries with Pear

This smoothie recipe is loved by children and adults alike.

Easy to prepare, light, and very healthy energetic berry cocktail with pear is perfect for breakfast or afternoon tea.

Ingredients

2 cups fresh or frozen blueberries

1 pear

½ cup cold water

1 1/2 cups low-fat yogurt (or low-calorie yogurt)

1-2 tbsp. spoons of honey

Instructions

Wash the pear, cut into four slices, remove the seeds.
Sort the fresh ripe blueberries carefully, wash in running water and remove the sepals.

If you are using frozen berries, rinse in warm water.

Combine all the ingredients (water, yogurt, honey, pear, and blueberry) and mix thoroughly in a blender for 3-5 minutes.

Your cocktail is ready to serve, bon appetit!

Blueberries & Banana

A blueberry smoothie is an unusually tasty and healthy drink.

Small blue-black berries are a natural storehouse of substances vital for the human body.

You should not deny yourself the pleasure of enjoying this wonderful cocktail, because in the summer it will not be difficult to buy fresh blueberries, and frozen ones are sold all year round in the supermarket.

Ingredients

1 cup blueberries (fresh or frozen)

1 banana

1/2 cup chilled milk (almond or rice can be used)

1 tbsp honey

3-4 ice cubes

Instructions

Put the sliced banana in a blender bowl along with the blueberries.

Beat the mixture until smooth, taste, and sweeten with honey if necessary.

Add the ice cubes and milk, beat again. Garnish with a mint leaf and fresh berries if desired.

You can diversify the recipe by taking a scoop of ice cream (creamy or vanilla) instead of ice.

Blueberries & Oatmeal

A blueberry smoothie is one of the most delicious breakfasts.

It is rich in oatmeal, banana, and berries with yogurt which provides the necessary energy.

A fresh banana can also be used to make a smoothie, but a frozen banana gives an airy texture when whisked with a blender.

Be sure to delight your loved ones with this smoothie!

Ingredients

1 cup blueberries (fresh or frozen)
1/2 cup milk (can be substituted with soy, almond, or other)
1 glass of natural yogurt
1 banana (frozen)
2-3 tablespoons of instant oatmeal
1/2 teaspoon lemon zest
2-3 pieces of ice (optional)
A few mint leaves (for decoration)

Instructions

Grind the oatmeal almost into flour.
Place the blueberries in a blender bowl. Add the milk and natural yogurt to it.

Peel the frozen banana and chop it into large chunks so you can grind it into a smoothie (you can use a fresh banana, but then add 2-3 pieces of ice to the smoothie to cool the smoothie).

Then add the oatmeal and lemon zest.
Mix everything well with a blender until smooth.

Serve with blueberries and mint.
Bon Appetit!

Cranberry & Oatmeal

The bright red ripe cranberries have unique properties.

Half a glass of cranberries contains the daily intake of vitamins C, A, E, and K, a third of the daily intake of B vitamins, as well as vitamin PP, which simulates the absorption of vitamin C in the body.

In addition to vitamins, the berry is rich in iron and trace elements such as potassium, phosphorus, calcium, etc.

Due to their composition, cranberries can increase immunity, have a general strengthening effect, and maintain health and strength.

Ingredients

1.5 cups cranberries

1 banana

2 tbsp oatmeal

2 cups yogurt

1 tsp honey – to taste

Instructions

Grind the oatmeal almost into flour.

Combine the oatmeal with 1 glass of yogurt and let it brew for 15-20 minutes.

Rinse and dry the cranberries, peel and cut the banana into slices, put in a blender bowl. Beat for 1 minute.

Add the oatmeal, glass of yogurt, and honey. Stir until smooth.

Pour into glasses and enjoy!

Cranberry & Apple

This smoothie recipe includes very affordable ingredients: some apples, a handful of cranberries, honey for sweetness, and ground cinnamon for piquancy.

The result is a pleasant sweet and sour drink, which is almost as useful as cranberry juice in the winter cold, and the taste is not inferior to the magic, slightly melted ice cream.

Ingredients

1/2 cup cranberries (fresh or frozen)

1 large apple (or 2-3 small ones)

1 cup natural or soy yogurt

1-2 tsp honey or any other sweetener

A pinch of ground cinnamon

Instructions

Peel the apples, remove the core and seeds, cut them into large pieces, and place them in the blender bowl.

Rinse the cranberries well, add to a blender.
Add the yogurt, honey, and the finishing touch: ground cinnamon.

Turn the blender on full power and beat the ingredients until a smooth smoothie is obtained.

Pour the finished drink into beautiful glasses, put a colored straw in each one and enjoy the incredible freshness.

Ginger Cranberry

Cranberries are a valuable forest gift that gives health, prolongs youth, and protects against flu and colds in the cold season.

Eating vitamin-rich cranberries is an excellent prevention of vitamin deficiency.

And in case of a cold, cranberry with honey relieves fever and gives strength, acts as an antibiotic, helping the body to cope with the disease faster.

Ingredients

1/2 cup frozen cranberries

1 sweet apple

1 grapefruit or orange

1/2 lemon

1-2 tablespoons honey

A small piece of fresh ginger

1/2 cup of still mineral water

Instructions

Core a sweet apple, peel, and cut into small cubes. Peel the grapefruit or orange, divide it into slices, cut off the thin white film from them. If you do not remove this film, the taste of the drink will be bitter.

Peel a small piece of fresh ginger, cut into thin strips, add to the grapefruit and apple. You need very little ginger for one serving of the drink - go too far with it and the cocktail will be sharp and even bitter, so two thin slices are enough.

Wash the cranberries, add to the fruit without defrosting - they will replace the ice in the drink.

Squeeze fresh lemon juice. To prevent the lemon seeds from entering the cocktail, strain the juice through a fine sieve.

Add the honey. Add about 1/2 cup of mineral water without gas to the ingredients, if there is none, then replace it with ordinary chilled boiled water.

Grind the ingredients with a blender until smooth, about 1 minute.

Fill the glasses with the bright drink and serve immediately.

Cranberries & Raspberries

This drink contains twice as many vitamins and antioxidants! This smoothie perfectly helps with colds and increases the protective functions of the body.

The smoothie turns out moderately sour, with a pleasant creamy texture.

Ingredients

1/2 cup cranberries

1/2 cup raspberries

1 ripe banana

2-5 dates

2 cups apple juice (or water)

A small piece of ginger root

Instructions

The berries can be fresh or frozen. Adjust the number of dates to taste, or replace with your favorite sweetener.

Wash the raspberries and cranberries, removing debris and spoiled berries. Peel the banana, cut it into circles. Remove the seeds from the dates.

Rub the ginger root on a fine grater. Put all of the ingredients in a blender bowl, add apple juice or water.

Grind all of the ingredients in a blender until smooth.

Your smoothie with raspberries and cranberries is ready, bon appetit!

Cranberries & Ginger

Cranberries lend a tart sweetness to any smoothie, and when paired with delicious ginger, there's no end to the amazing depth of flavors.

Ingredients

2 cups cranberries

1 tablespoon grated ginger

1 cup vanilla rice milk

¼ cup ice

Instructions

Sort the fresh ripe cranberries carefully, wash in running water, and remove the sepals.
If you are using frozen berries, rinse in warm water.

In a blender, combine the cranberries, ginger, and rice milk with ¼ cup ice, and blend until thoroughly combined.

Peach & Apricot Smoothies

Juicy, aromatic, sweet, with tender pulp, peaches and apricots are liked by almost everyone. Peaches and apricots are some of the most delicious and healthy summer fruits. These fruits are a real treat for lovers of juicy and sweet, and this makes peaches and apricots stand out from all other representatives of the fruit kingdom. Peaches and apricots are among the leaders in the content of vitamins and minerals in their composition among all other fruits.

Almost all varieties of peaches are very similar in appearance, the only exception is the fig peach. It resembles a fig in shape and differs from its counterparts in that its white, very sweet pulp separates well from the peach seed.

But "bald peaches" - nectarines - are obtained by crossing ordinary peaches with plums. Nectarines have a smooth bone that separates easily from the pulp and a sweet, pleasant taste.

Peach is not only excellent for refreshing, but also a useful medicine. The benefits of peaches lie in their diuretic effect, they lower blood pressure, reduce the risk of stroke, cleanse the body, and stimulate and facilitate digestion.

Peaches contain antioxidants like beta-carotene, vitamin C, and selenium, which help the body fight free radicals. In addition, peaches have a beneficial effect on the functioning of the digestive system, thyroid gland and protect the heart.

The benefits of peaches for depression, fatigue, and nervousness are known.

Apricots are good for the cardiovascular system and normalize blood pressure. This fruit is a source of iron, potassium, and magnesium. Apricots are very useful for hypertensive patients, as well as people with kidney disease. Apricots should be used for atherosclerosis and circulatory system problems.

Apricots contain a lot of fiber, which normalizes the digestion process and removes harmful substances from the body. Eating apricots will help lower cholesterol and improve intestinal microflora. The fruits contain a lot of vitamin A, which is necessary for vision and facial skin.

Cooking features

Smoothies can be made not only from fresh peaches but also from frozen ones, even from canned ones. The canned product is less useful and has a sweeter taste, therefore it is suitable only for smoothies prepared for dessert and for those who do not need to count calories.

If you are slimming, only fresh or frozen fruits are good for you.

Frozen peaches are taken out of the refrigerator in advance so that they have time to thaw. Fresh ones must be washed, preferably in warm water, dried by blotting with a towel, cut in half and take out the stone, and then cut into small pieces. There is no need to peel peaches before dipping in a blender.

The balanced sweet and sour taste of peaches and their juicy, but dense structure allow you to combine them with any berries and fruits, regardless of their taste and texture. If necessary, ready-made smoothies are diluted with kefir or natural yogurt, or fruit juice.

By adding ice cream or cream to the smoothie, you increase the calorie content of the drink. Refuse such options if you have problems with your weight.

Peach smoothies can be substituted for a snack. Eat it in small spoonfuls, and then the satiety will come faster.

Peach & Banana

The combination of peach, banana, and yogurt is a win-win combination, and the taste of such a drink turns out to be delicate and pleasant, and a beautifully decorated smoothie pleases the eye with its sunny appearance.

Natural yogurt in this recipe can be replaced with kefir, soy yogurt, or milk (plain or almond).

Ingredients

2 ripe peaches + a few pieces to garnish

1 banana

2/3 cup natural unsweetened yogurt

Honey or another sweetener to taste

A few mint leaves

Instructions

Peel the bananas and cut them into medium-thick circles. Freeze the bananas for a refreshing smoothie.

While the bananas are freezing, prepare the peaches. Wash them well and pat dry with a towel. Many people believe that it is better to cut off the velvety skin so that its unmilled pieces do not come across in the finished drink. Cut the flesh of the peaches into small pieces.

Place the frozen bananas and peach slices into a blender bowl, fill with natural yogurt, add honey and a few mint leaves.

Whisk the ingredients well with a blender until smooth.

Peaches & Cherries

This light fruit smoothie made from peach, cherry, and yogurt is a nutritious, healthy, and tasty drink that will be enjoyed by children and adults.

A great option for a healthy treat for a children's party or a light snack. Try it!

Ingredients

2 fig peach

1 apple

1 cup pitted cherries

1 cup natural yogurt

1 tbsp nuts (almonds or peanuts) - to taste and desire or 1 tbsp. cereals

Instructions

Put the nuts into a blender bowl and grind them into flour. (Nuts can be substituted with 1 tablespoon of rolled oats.)

Cut the peach pulp from the stone and, together with the apple and cherry pieces, add to the blender bowl, pour in a little yogurt, and beat everything well.

Add the remaining yogurt and beat again.

Ice Peach

Simplicity is the key to perfection, and this smoothie is definitely simple!

When you combine sweet peaches with a mild banana flavor, you have a flavorful smoothie that will make you fresh and cool any time of the day!

Ingredients

2 cups peaches

1 banana, peeled

½ cup of water

½ cup of ice

Instructions

Peel the bananas and cut them into medium-thick circles. Freeze the bananas for a refreshing smoothie.

Wash the peaches well and pat dry with a towel. Many people believe that it is better to cut off the velvety skin so that its unmilled pieces do not come across in the finished drink. Cut the flesh of the peaches into small pieces.

In a blender, combine the peaches, banana, and water with ½ cup ice and beat until smooth.

While mixing, add the remaining ice until the desired consistency is achieved.

Apricot & Peach

This Apricot and Peach Smoothie is an exquisite dessert that can bring true delight.

It's aromatic and sweet even without added sugar or other sweeteners.

Ingredients

- 8 Apricots
- 2 Peaches
- 1 Banana
- 1 Lemon
- 2 cups Freshly squeezed orange juice

Instructions

Squeeze the juice out of the lemon. Squeeze the juice out of the oranges for the base, or use the ready-made sugar-free juice with pulp.

Peel and break the banana into large pieces.

Place apricots, peach, and banana halves in a blender and cover with orange juice and half the freshly squeezed lemon juice.

Mix all of the ingredients in a blender at high speed.

Check the sweet to sour ratio (depending on how sweet the apricots and peaches were), add the juice of the second half of the lemon if necessary, and stir again.

Apricot & Strawberry

Delicious, bright, filled with wonderful aroma and vitamins, this simple layered cocktail combines the brightest flavors of summer.

This smoothie is a great breakfast or healthy snack for the whole family. Regular milk in this smoothie can be easily replaced with plant-based milk (soy milk, nuts, cereal, coconut).

Ingredients

1 cup chopped apricots

1/2 peach

1 cup strawberries

1 banana

1 cup milk (you can use soy or nut milk)

2 teaspoons honey

Instructions

Pour half the milk (1/2 cup) into the blender bowl.

Wash the apricots well, halve them and remove the seeds. Throw the pulp together with the skin into the milk, add ½ part of the peach there. Sweeten with 1 tsp honey. Beat on high speed until smooth.

Half fill a glass with the apricot smoothie.

Rinse the strawberries in running water, dry them a little and remove the stalks. Peel the banana.

In a blender, combine the remaining milk with the strawberries and banana. You can use frozen berries directly from the freezer. Add a spoonful of honey and whisk the mixture at high speed. To accentuate the sweetness of the fruit, you can add some freshly squeezed lemon or lime juice to the layer of the strawberry-banana smoothie.

Gently pour a layer of strawberry over the apricot portion of the smoothie. Serve with a teaspoon or wide-bore cocktail straw.

Apricots & Orange

Delicate, fragrant, juicy apricots rightfully take prizes among the most delicious fruits.

And a large amount of vitamins and minerals makes them extremely beneficial.

Ingredients

- 3 apricots
- 1 orange
- 1.5 cups natural yogurt
- 2 tablespoons honey

Instructions

Chill the yogurt beforehand. Put the fruit in the refrigerator half an hour before cooking.

Peel the orange, cut it into wedges, remove the seeds and inner films. Wash the apricots well, halve them and remove the seeds.

Grind the fruit pulp with a blender together with honey. Add chilled yogurt, beat well.

Pour the smoothie into glasses and serve immediately.

Apricot & Banana

Apricots contain a significant amount of nutrients: pectin, inulin, dextrin, organic acids. The aromatic fruits also contain vitamin C and beta-carotene, so they are good for the eyes, thyroid, and liver.

This Apricot Banana Smoothie is a delicious, thick, and refreshing drink.

On a hot summer day, it will perfectly quench your thirst and fill the body with vitamins.

Ingredients

5 large ripe apricots

1 banana

1 glass of milk (you can almond, any nut, or soy)

1 sprig of mint

Instructions

Wash the apricots, divide them in half and remove the pits. Peel the banana (it is better to choose overripe), break into pieces or cut it into pieces.

Transfer the fruit to a blender bowl. Pour chilled milk in. Add a few mint leaves for flavor.

Turn the blender to maximum and beat the fruit until smooth.

Pour the apricot smoothie into tall glasses or goblets, top with a straw and a sprig of mint.

Bon Appetit!

Apple & Pear Smoothies

Apples are among the most readily available fruits. They can be purchased in the store at any time of the year. Because of this, some people treat apples with a certain disdain, preferring exotic fruits. The apple deserves respect, as it contains especially many vitamins and other elements that are not always found in other fruits, at least in such quantities.

Apples are justifiably called the fruits of health. In addition to a large number of vitamins, they contain manganese, potassium, and iron. They are used to stabilize pressure and strengthen bone tissue and tooth enamel. Pectin, which is part of the fruit, improves complexion and prolongs the youthfulness of the skin.

Apples are useful for gout, rheumatism, eczema, and joint diseases. Apples also help fight iron deficiency anemia, as they contain a lot of iron, strengthen the immune system due to a fairly high content of vitamin C. Therefore, apple smoothies are not only tasty but also healthy.

Pear smoothies have a seductive sweetish but at the same time fresh aroma, pleasant taste. Both children and adults drink them with pleasure.

Pears are high in potassium and iron, antioxidants, and mood-enhancing substances. Pears are known for their tonic, diuretic, disinfectant, antipyretic and expectorant properties. The fruits contain a natural antibiotic that destroys harmful microorganisms found in the kidneys, intestines, and gallbladder. Eating these sweet fruits will help normalize the digestion process, strengthen blood vessels and heart muscle, and cure colds and bronchitis.

A pear smoothie has a delicate texture, is easy to drink, quenches thirst, and relieves hunger.

Cooking features

The most delicious is a cocktail made from several varieties of apples.

The most delicious and aromatic drink comes from juicy, fully ripe pears with a soft texture.

Apples and pears are usually peeled, as this will make the cocktail more tender. However, if you are interested in making the drink not only tasty but also healthy, an apple and a pear for it can be chopped without peeling. But the seedboxes from the fruit must be cut out in any case.

The apple smoothie will turn out to be delicious even if it is not cool. However, if you add crushed ice to it, it turns into a refreshing drink that quenches your thirst well on hot days.

Antioxidant-rich fruit drinks such as pears should be consumed immediately after preparation for maximum benefits. You should not prepare a large amount of pear smoothie for future use, especially since it does not take a lot of time to prepare it.

Spices and herbs will not only improve the taste of the smoothie but also enhance its weight loss benefits, as they help speed up the metabolism.

So that the chopped apples do not darken for as long as possible, they are sprinkled with lemon juice. This method is best suited for sweet varieties of apples, which, when combined with lemon juice, acquire a more refined taste.

If you have apples of sweet and sour varieties at your disposal, it is better to prepare a mixture of lemon juice and boiled water, taking no more than a tablespoon of juice per half liter of water. Apple slices are dipped in acidified water, kept in it for about a minute and thrown into a colander.

Instead of lemon, you can take lime, its juice has the same properties. If there is neither one nor the other, you can use a solution of citric acid by dissolving a teaspoon of the powder in a liter of water.

Apple, Pear & Basil

Pear is rightfully considered one of the most useful and valuable fruits for humans. The pear does not cause allergies, which is rare for a fruit.

This delicious smoothie will help you cope with vitamin deficiencies and improve your mood. To add a light refreshing touch to the drink, add a little green basil.

Ingredients

2 sweet and sour apples

2 pears

1-2 sprigs of green basil

1/3 cup apple juice (or water)

Ice (optional)

Instructions

Wash the fruit, peel, and remove the seeds, cut the fruits into pieces. Rinse basil in running water, shake off excess moisture, chop finely.

Combine the apples and pears with the chopped basil leaves in a blender.

Add crushed ice if desired. Whisk all the ingredients until a smooth consistency is achieved.

If the smoothie is too thick, dilute it with mineral water or apple juice and whisk again in a blender.

Apple & Banana

This simple and sweet smoothie combines the familiar and favorite flavors of apples and bananas and turns them into a cool, icy treat.

Ideal for people in a rush in the morning. You don't have to give up a good breakfast because it can be prepared very quickly!

Ingredients

1 red or yellow apple with a core

1 banana, peeled

1 cup of natural, organic apple juice (not from concentrate)

1/3 cup of ice

Instructions

Wash the apple, peel, and remove the seeds, cut the fruits into pieces.

Peel the banana, break into pieces or cut it into pieces.

In a blender, combine the banana, apple, and apple juice with 1/3 cup ice and beat until smooth.

While stirring, add the remaining ice until the desired consistency is achieved.

Apple & Mango

A refreshing smoothie made from aromatic apples and juicy mangoes. Mango gives the drink a unique taste that cannot be compared with anything else.

This drink will perfectly quench your thirst and cheer you up even on a cloudy day!

Ingredients

2 apples

1/2 mango

1/2 cup apple juice

A few ice cubes optional

Instructions

Peel the mango and cut it into cubes.
Peel the apples, core them, and then cut them into slices.

Place the mango and apple slices in a blender bowl, add the apple juice, and beat the ingredients for 2 minutes. To chill the smoothie, add a few ice cubes and beat again.

Pour the finished mango and apple smoothie into a tall glass, garnish with berries or attach a piece of mango to the edge of the glass and serve.

Bon Appetite!

Savory Apple & Pear

The sweet and unique flavor of delicious pears is combined with apples and the aromatic blend of spicy ginger, cloves, and cardamom for a heightened sensual experience all swirled up in a nutritious smoothie.

Ingredients

2 large apples
1 large, juicy and sweet pear
1/2 lemon or lime
1 teaspoon ground ginger
1 teaspoon clove, ground
1 teaspoon ground cardamom
1/2 cup of water
1/3 cup of ice
honey to taste

Instructions

Remove the core and peel the apples and pears, cut into pieces. Add lemon or lime juice.

In a blender, combine the apples, pears, ginger, cloves, cardamom, and 1/2 cup water with 1/3 cup ice and beat until smooth.

While stirring, add water or ice until the desired consistency is achieved.

If it's not sweet enough for you, add honey to taste.

Apple, Banana & Oatmeal

If you don't have time to prepare breakfast, make a healthy morning oatmeal smoothie.

Fiber-rich oatmeal is ideal for preparing a healthy meal. The apple banana oat smoothie is a great breakfast any time of the year.

The drink is rich in antioxidants and gives a powerful boost of vivacity and energy.

Ingredients

1 apple

1 banana

2 tbsp oatmeal

1 glass of yogurt

honey or maple syrup - to taste

Instructions

Soak the flakes in half of the yogurt for at least an hour.

Peel, core, and dice the apple. Cut the banana into small pieces.

Place the fruit in a blender, top with yogurt, add cinnamon, honey, or syrup, and beat well.

When the mass becomes homogeneous, add the soaked flakes to it. Stir again.

Apples & Spices

Stuffed with apples and delicious spices, this frosty smoothie will surely make you think of a delicious apple pie.

And the original combination of spices will give you an unforgettable pleasure!

Ingredients

2 red apples without a core

1 teaspoon ground cinnamon

1 teaspoon clove, ground

1 teaspoon ground ginger

1 cup all natural, organic apple juice (not from concentrate)

1/3 cup of ice

Instructions

Peel, core, and dice the apple.

In a blender, combine the apples, cinnamon, cloves, ginger, and apple juice with 1/3 cup ice and beat until smooth.

While stirring, add the remaining ice until the desired consistency is achieved.

Apple & Lemon

If you're not a big fan of lemons, this recipe is the perfect way to lighten the taste of this yellow fruit.

Lemons and sweet apples are perfectly balanced in this smoothie.

You will enjoy a delicious smoothie packed with nutrients that will refresh your body and mind!

Ingredients

2 yellow or green apples without a core

1 cup organic apple juice (not from concentrate)

2 lemons, peeled and seeded

½ glass of ice

honey or maple syrup (optional)

Instructions

Wash the apple, peel, and remove the seeds, cut the fruits into pieces.

In a blender, combine the lemons, apples, and apple juice with ½ cup ice and beat until smooth.

While stirring, add the remaining ice until the desired consistency is achieved.

If the drink is too sour for you, add some honey or maple syrup.

Pear & Ginger

The combination of pear and ginger is the perfect combination for strengthening the immune system.

A thick, rich and slightly spicy pear and ginger smoothie is the right choice for your morning drink at the start of the week.
You can drink it both cold and warm.

Ingredients

2 pears

1/3 teaspoon grated ginger root

1.5 cups almond milk

1 tablespoon maple syrup or honey

3 tablespoon hemp seeds

Instructions

Wash the pear, peel, cut into pieces and transfer to a blender bowl. Peel and grate the ginger root.

Add the almond milk and honey and beat until smooth.

To make a warm smoothie, whisk the ingredients in a blender on full power for 2-3 minutes, or use warm almond milk or microwave to finish the drink.

Mint Pear

This smoothie can be a great breakfast or snack - light, nutritious and healthy.

Mint will give a charge of freshness for a vigorous morning.

Ingredients

4 pears

1 large bunch of seedless green grapes

7-8 sprigs of fresh mint

3 table. spoons of honey

Freshly squeezed juice and zest of 1 lime

1/2 cup sparkling water

Instructions

Freeze the grapes in advance.

Separate the mint leaves from the stems and chop.

Place the peeled pears, lime zest, frozen grapes, honey, and mint in a blender and beat for about 30-40 seconds.

Add lime juice, top up with soda water, and serve.

Pear & Spices

Enjoy the invigorating aroma of a fresh pear smoothie.

This very simple recipe is packed with delicious cinnamon and vanilla aromas.

Ingredients

1 pear (diced)
1 banana (ripe, chopped)
2/3 cup almond milk
2-4 slices of ginger (fresh, peeled)
2 tablespoons honey or agave nectar
1/2 teaspoon vanilla extract
1/2 tablespoon cinnamon (ground)
1/2 cup ice

Instructions

Peel the banana and pear cut them into pieces.

In a blender, combine the banana, pear, almond milk, ginger, honey, vanilla extract, and ground cinnamon. Add ice, stir again.

Instead of fresh ginger, you can use 1 teaspoon of ground ginger.

In warm weather, avoid adding cinnamon and ginger. Instead, add 1 tablespoon of rosemary and a few tablespoons of freshly squeezed orange juice.

Cherry & Sweet Cherry Smoothies

Summer is the best time to cook all sorts of goodies with cherries and cherries. I always look forward to the cherry season. Today, in the markets and stores, you can buy any kind of sweet cherries - sweeter, less sweet, red-black cherries, cherries with a pink tint, yellow cherries, sweet or sour-sweet cherries, and of course ripe cherries.

And what smoothies are obtained from these berries - bright, rich, and incredibly tasty. Be sure to try making sweet cherry and cherry smoothies and they will captivate you with their taste.

What is the difference between cherry and sweet cherry? Mostly taste.

Due to their rich and tart taste, cherries are better suited for preserving and preparing various dishes, but sweet cherries are best eaten fresh.

Despite the difference in taste, both berries are very healthy. Although cherries contain more vitamins, both fruits are on an equal footing in the number of antioxidants.

Cherries and sweet cherries are low in calories. Fresh, these berries have approximately the same calorie content of 50-62 kcal. Cherries are the champion of the low glycemic index among fruits, it is equal to 22. In sweet cherries, the index is also low - 25.

Cherries and sweet cherries contain macro-and microelements: potassium, calcium, iron, magnesium, silicon, and others, as well as dietary plant fibers: pectins, fiber, which is 5-8% of the daily value.

Cherries, especially tart sour varieties, contain melatonin - a hormone that improves sleep and has an antidepressant effect.

Sweet cherry is very useful for diseases of the heart and blood vessels, it helps to thin the blood, and also cleanses it of "bad" cholesterol. For everyone who leads a sedentary lifestyle and disappears for hours in the office, juicy cherries will serve as a good prevention of varicose veins and blood stagnation. Moreover, sweet cherries are good for anyone who suffers from joint pain, especially with osteoarthritis and gout.
Sweet cherry contains a huge number of powerful antioxidants that slow down cell aging and have a rejuvenating and cleansing effect. It also helps to rid the body of toxins, normalizes the liver and kidneys. By cleansing the body of dirt and toxins, cherries have a positive effect on skin health and improve complexion.

Bright sweet cherries also have a beneficial effect on the digestive system, help to normalize metabolism, and improve appetite and food absorption.

A very important quality of the berry is a low content of organic acids, so those who suffer from gastritis, stomach ulcers, and high acidity can also eat sweet cherries.

How to store cherries

Cherries and cherries are fairly perishable foods. Warm temperatures are their main enemy. Nutritionists say that cherries lose as many nutrients in one hour at room temperature as in one day in the refrigerator. For this reason, try to put the cherries in the refrigerator as soon as possible after purchase.

It is important to remember that you do not need to wash your cherries before placing them in the refrigerator, as this will spoil them faster. Wash cherries just before eating or preserving.

How to remove cherry pits quickly

If you need to quickly remove pits from cherries, and there is no special machine for pitting at hand, then this can be done using a regular bottle and stick, straw, wooden skewer, or a regular toothpick. Place the cherry on the neck of the bottle and squeeze out the pit with a skewer.

This method will undoubtedly work if you need to process a small number of cherries, say, for a pie or cherry smoothie, but if you are waiting for a whole bucket of berries, it is better to buy yourself a cherry pitting tool.

Sweet Cherry & Oatmeal

This sweet cherry smoothie is a tasty and healthy drink that retains all the beneficial properties of berries, strengthening the immune system, improving the cardiovascular and digestive systems.

Such a thick cocktail perfectly quenches thirst and hunger, and the taste and aroma will not leave anyone indifferent.

Ingredients

- 1 cup sweet cherry
- 1-2 tbsp instant oatmeal
- 1 cup milk (you can use soy or nut milk) or yogurt
- 1 tsp honey
- 1 pinch cinnamon

Instructions

Remove the pits from the cherries.

Pour the oatmeal into milk or yogurt and let it sit for 10-15 minutes. Melt the honey.

Place the cherries and oatmeal in a blender, pour the honey on top. Convert the ingredients into a homogeneous mass.

Pour the finished cocktail into a tall glass and sprinkle with cinnamon.

Cherries & Spice

Creamy, spicy, and sweet, this smoothie is a delicious way to pack in some nutritious fruit servings.

This tasty recipe takes healthy living to a whole new level!

Ingredients

2 cups cherries, pitted
1 tablespoon grated ginger
1 teaspoon ground cloves
1 teaspoon ground nutmeg
1 cup vanilla almond milk
1 cup ice
½ cup water

Instructions

Remove the pits from the cherries.

In a blender, combine the cherries, ginger, cloves, nutmeg, and almond milk with ½ cup ice, and blend until thoroughly combined.

While blending, add the water and remaining ice until desired consistency is achieved.

Sweet Cherries & Strawberries

This sweet cherry and strawberry smoothie is a colorful, healthy, and tasty drink that will pleasantly diversify your daily menu and add more natural vitamins to your diet. Made with yogurt and vanilla, this smoothie comes out fragrant, nutritious, and very appetizing in appearance and taste.

Great for a healthy snack or light breakfast that can be prepared in minutes.

Ingredients

- 1 cup sweet cherries
- 1 cup strawberries (fresh or frozen)
- 1 glass of natural yogurt
- A pinch of vanilla
- 1-2 tsp honey (optional)

Instructions

Pre-chill the yogurt.

Wash the fresh strawberries, peel the sepals. Remove the pits from the cherries.

Place the berries in a blender bowl and cover with yogurt. Beat until smooth.

If you are lacking in sweetness, add 1-2 teaspoons of honey.

Add the vanilla in and beat again.

Pour into tall glasses and serve.

Cherries & Chocolate

This sweet cherry smoothie is a tasty and healthy soft drink that retains all the beneficial properties of the berries.

The taste and aroma of the drink will definitely not leave anyone indifferent. Such a thick cocktail perfectly quenches thirst and hunger, so it can easily replace unhealthy snacks.

Ingredients

1 cup sweet cherries
1/2 cup sugar-free yogurt (or almond milk)
1 tablespoon cocoa powder or grated dark chocolate
1 teaspoon honey (or 1 large date)
1 pinch cinnamon
1/4 cup ice

Instructions

Mix cocoa powder with a small amount of yogurt and beat thoroughly until a homogeneous mass without lumps is formed. Then add the remaining yogurt and beat.

Peel the cherries. Melt the honey. Instead of honey, you can add 1 large date. Put the cherries and yogurt with the cocoa in a blender bowl and pour in the honey. Grind the ingredients.

Add crushed ice, beat for 10-15 seconds.

Sprinkle with ground cinnamon before serving.

Cherry, Apple & Banana

A recipe for a delicious cherry smoothie with mint and cinnamon, which you simply cannot help but fall in love with.

Treat yourself and your household with this homemade delicacy and you will never again want milkshakes from cafes and restaurants.

Ingredients

- 1 cup frozen pitted cherries
- 1 apple
- 1 banana
- 1 cup natural yogurt without additives
- 2-3 sprigs of mint
- 0.5 tsp ground cinnamon

Instructions

Cherries can be used fresh or frozen for this smoothie. Fresh fruits must be washed, then the seeds must be removed from them.

Pitted frozen cherries do not need to be defrosted beforehand, as this drink is best served chilled. Pour the prepared cherries into a blender.

Peel the banana, remove the core from the apple. Tear off the leaves from the mint, we don't need the twigs. Cut the fruit into slices. Add to blender bowl, stir. Add yogurt and cinnamon.

Pulse the ingredients in a high-speed blender until they are well combined.

Piquant Cherry with Basil

This recipe is a find of the last cherry season! In the hot season, it will perfectly quench your thirst, tones, refreshes, and give strength. The combination of cherry and basil is surprisingly harmonious.

The only advice is to choose riper cherries, as they have a less characteristic sourness.

However, the benefits of ripe, almost black cherries are much greater! The darker the berry, the more iron and natural antioxidants it contains.

Ingredients

1 cup of cherries

1-2 sprigs of dark basil

1 tablespoon lemon juice

1-2 tablespoons honey or any other sweetener (optional)

1/2 cup water or yogurt

Instructions

Wash the cherries, basil, and lemon. Take out the seeds from the berries and add the cherries to the blender bowl.

Separate the basil leaves from the stem. We only need the aroma, so we take the most delicate leaves. If you're not sure if you'll like it, grab some basil.

Grind the herbs a little and add to the cherries.

Squeeze out the lemon juice. If the berries are very sour, then lemon juice can be replaced with grated zest - the aroma will remain, but there will be no excess acid. Add honey and yogurt.

Beat all components of the smoothie with a blender at high speed. Continue to beat for a few more minutes until smooth.

Pour into glasses and enjoy the smoothie.

Cherries, Banana & Coconut

If you're like most people, cherries splits bring back memories of carefree childhood bliss.

Here, instead of using processed ice cream and additives, this smoothie uses all-natural ingredients that are packed full of B vitamins and vitamin C.

Ingredients

¼ cup cherries, pitted

2 bananas, peeled

½ cup coconut meat

1 cup plain yogurt

½ cup water

½ cup ice

Instructions

Cherries can be used fresh or frozen for this smoothie. Fresh fruits must be washed, then the seeds must be removed from them.

Pitted frozen cherries do not need to be defrosted beforehand, as this drink is best served chilled. Pour the prepared cherries into a blender.

Peel the banana and pear cut them into pieces.

In a blender, combine the bananas, coconut meat, cherries, plain yogurt, and ½ cup water with ½ cup ice, and blend until thoroughly combined.

While blending, add the remaining water and ice until the desired consistency is achieved.

Ginger Cherry

Try a cherry smoothie with a spicy touch of ginger. This is an excellent snack, juicy, with a bright taste and delicate structure.

It is prepared in a matter of minutes, but it will bring you real pleasure!

Ingredients

1 cup pitted cherries (fresh or frozen)

1/2 cup almond or soy milk (or yogurt)

1 teaspoon lemon or lime juice 1 tbsp honey (to taste)

1 teaspoon grated ginger root

1 teaspoon chia or flax seeds (optional)

Instructions

Wash the cherries, remove the seeds, put them in the blender bowl.

Add the vegetable milk or natural yogurt, then add fresh ginger grated on a fine grater, pour in lemon juice and honey.

Add flax seeds (can be pre-ground in a coffee grinder) or chia seeds.

Stir with a blender until smooth. Enjoy!

Tropical Fruit Smoothie

We have all become accustomed to oranges and tangerines for a long time, even bananas and mango have ceased to be something special for us. You can buy the most exotic fruits today without any problems. The variety of such fruits amazes the imagination and excites our taste buds.

So why not please yourself and your loved ones with a fragrant, tasty, beautiful, and healthy tropical fruit smoothie?

This drink contains an incredible amount of vitamins and will give you a boost of vivacity and a good mood!

The benefits of exotic fruits are due to their rich composition. Tropical fruits are juicy, aromatic, mostly sweet, sometimes with a pleasant sourness or more neutral. They are not only tasty and interesting in appearance, but are also recommended for use by doctors.

Kiwi

Just one kiwi provides the body with double the daily intake of vitamin C. This means that kiwi lovers are not threatened with autumn colds, infections, and premature aging. Kiwi can burn fat that blocks arteries, which reduces the risk of blood clots. However, it is worth remembering that kiwi often causes allergic reactions.

That is why doctors do not recommend giving this fruit to children under 5 years old. When choosing a kiwi, lightly press down on it with your finger. If the fruit is soft, then it is fully ripe.

Passion fruit

Cleans the body of toxins, it is recommended for hypotonic patients, and people with liver and kidney diseases. However, the main value of passionfruit is its delicate, incomparable aroma. Thanks to it, passion fruit is called the fruit of passion.

Pineapple

Contains a large number of B vitamins (necessary for the well-coordinated work of the nervous system, health of the skin and hair), potassium (needed for the heart and blood vessels), iron (promotes the supply of oxygen to tissues), magnesium (strengthens the nerves and relieves muscle cramps), zinc (makes the skin elastic and the hair thick).

Pineapple improves digestion, dulls hunger, and removes excess fluid from the body. Thanks to these properties, it is often recommended for those who want to get rid of extra pounds. Pineapple is useful for hypertensive patients. Due to its diuretic effect, this fruit quickly lowers blood pressure. Ripe pineapple has yellowish skin and a sweetish smell. However, the aroma should not be too strong - if the pineapple smells too harsh, this indicates the beginning of the fermentation process.

Papaya

contains a lot of vitamins A and C, as well as twice as much potassium as bananas. This is the best fruit for those who are on a diet: firstly, it is tasty and sweet, secondly, it contains a lot of nutrients and only 28 calories, and thirdly, it helps to remove excess fluid from the body, which further contributes to weight loss ...

Papaya contains a unique enzyme called papain, which aids digestion and suppresses most E. coli. Papaya is also useful for those who suffer from heartburn and gastritis.

Mango

is a real gift for those who want to keep their eyesight sharp and their skin elastic - in terms of beta-carotene content, its sweet pulp surpasses the usual carrots. In addition to vitamin A, mango contains B vitamins, a lot of potassium, and iron. Mango fruits have a mild laxative effect, they improve digestion and kidney function. Sometimes mangoes are used as a remedy for insomnia. Well, for those who suffer from gastritis with high acidity, it is recommended to drink mango juice more often, which soothes the inflamed gastric mucosa.

Kiwi & Mango

An amazingly simple and tasty drink with a bright aroma of tropical fruits.

The banana and kiwi smoothie turns out to be satisfying and you can even take such a smoothie with you in a special glass and drink it on the way to work.

Ingredients

3 kiwis

1 mango

1 banana

2 cups pineapple juice

Instructions

Peel the kiwis, mango, and banana and cut them into slices.

Whisk the fruit in a blender along with the pineapple juice.

Enjoy!

Creamy Kiwi

    I love the banana and kiwi smoothie because these two ingredients are not seasonal and are available in our stores all year round. This means that we can get our portion of vitamins even in winter when vitamins are especially needed.

    I do not add sugar to the drink, I replace it with honey, as a result of which the smoothie turns out to be even healthier.

Ingredients

3 kiwis

2 ripe bananas

1 cup of cream 10%

Honey - 2 tablespoons

Instructions

For a thick and refreshing smoothie, chill all the ingredients in the refrigerator well before cooking.

Peel and cut the fruit, beat in a blender. Add cream and honey, stir again. If you use very ripe fruits, you don't need to add honey.

Our banana kiwi smoothie is ready. It's incredibly tasty, plus it's also healthy!

Kiwi, Banana & Chia Seeds

Try this delicious and healthy kiwi, banana, and chia smoothie.

Kiwi is a boost of vitamin C, banana is for satiety and pleasure, chia seeds are a source of protein and a healthy superfood.

If you feel like adding sweetness, use agave syrup or honey.

Ingredients

3 kiwis

2 bananas

2 tablespoons chia seeds

1 cup of water

1 tablespoon of agave syrup or honey

Instructions

Cover the chia seeds with water and allow them to sit for 5 minutes, add them to the blender bowl.

Peel the kiwi and banana, cut into slices, add to the chia, stir.

Add agave syrup or honey, stir again.

Kiwi & Nectarine

I added a rather exotic fruit to this delicious fruit smoothie - the golden kiwi, which was first grown in New Zealand and recently hit our shelves. Unlike regular green kiwi, gold kiwi is bright yellow on the inside and almost bald on the outside, has a sweeter taste, and when combined with honey will make this smoothie a real gourmet treat.

Another exotic addition to refresh this smoothie is fresh rosemary. But use rosemary in moderation; just a few leaves can give your smoothie a strong spruce flavor.

Ingredients

2 golden kiwis (yellow)

1 nectarine

1 apple

Juice of half a lemon

1 tablespoon honey

Rosemary, mint - 1 small sprig each

A few ice cubes

Instructions

Wash the ripe nectarine thoroughly, remove the stone, cut it into thick slices, you can remove the skin from the nectarine.

Wash a ripe and sweet apple, peel, cut into small pieces.

Add two thick, peeled yellow kiwis to the fruit. Add honey to the fruit.

To avoid making the smoothie very thick and sweet-sweet, add freshly squeezed lemon juice to it.

A few fresh rosemary leaves will add sophistication to the smoothie, but don't overdo it with this aromatic spice. Even a small amount of rosemary (3-4 leaves) is enough to feel it in a cocktail.

Grind the fruit in a food processor or blender until pureed. If you like a thick smoothie, you can leave it as it is.

To cool the smoothie, you can add ice cubes to the fruit, or a little chilled mineral water without gas, or fruit juice without sugar, then you will get a very large portion of the drink.

Pour the smoothie into a cup or glass, serve immediately, garnish with a lemon wedge and fresh mint.

Mango Surprise

Whenever I miss the sun, I love to treat myself to a vibrant yellow mango orange smoothie.

This smoothie is great for energizing and will quickly cheer you up, especially on cloudy days.

This mouth-watering smoothie is super healthy, with a two-day dose of Vitamin C and Vitamin A.

Ingredients

- 1 mango
- 2 oranges
- 1 banana (fresh or frozen)
- 1 cup pineapple chunks (fresh or frozen)

Instructions

In this recipe, you can use either a whole orange (with or without internal baffles) or its juice.

If you want a softer smoothie texture, you must first juice two oranges.

If you are using a whole orange, simply peel it, remove the seeds, slice it and toss it into the blender bowl.

Peel the mango and cut it in half along the pit. Chop the pulp into random pieces and place it in a blender bowl on top of the orange.

Then, peel the banana and cut it into wedges. Add it to the rest of the ingredients.

Also, add the peeled pineapple pieces to the blender.

Whisk the fruit until smooth.

Pour the smoothie into glasses and serve.

Mango, Apple & Basil

Basil gives this smoothie a spicy flavor and aroma.

The original taste of the smoothie will impress even the most sophisticated gourmet.

Ingredients

1 mango
1 banana
1 apple
1 cups peeled and chopped pineapple
1 lemon
4 sprigs of basil
4-5 ice cubes

Instructions

Wash, peel, pit, and cut the mangoes. Peel bananas and pineapple and cut into slices.

Wash the apple, core with seeds, and cut into slices. Wash the basil, dry, and tear off the leaves. Wash the lemon, squeeze the juice.

Place the prepared mango, pineapple , banana, apple, basil, and lemon juice in a blender along with ice cubes and chop.

Pour into glasses, decorate with basil leaves.
You can decorate each serving with lemon slices.

Mango & Banana

If you can't remember the last time you enjoyed a mango, now is the time!

Not only is this vibrant fruit a great ingredient, but mango is also a rich source of Vitamin A, which promotes skin and eye health with every delicious, nutritious sip!

Ingredients

- 1 cup peeled mango
- 1 banana, peeled
- 1 cup coconut milk
- ½ glass of ice

Instructions

Wash, peel, pit, and cut the mangoes. Peel bananas and cut into slices.

In a blender, combine the mango, banana, and coconut milk with ½ cup ice and beat until smooth.

While stirring, add the remaining ice until the desired consistency is achieved.

Pineapple Delight

If you're in the mood for a tropical treat this smoothie is just perfect! Real pineapple, citrus, and coconut blend together with creamy coconut milk and crushed ice for a frothy glow.

You'll feel like you've landed in paradise. The drink umbrella is optional, but go for it if you want to take things up a notch!

Ingredients

1 cup pineapple

½ lemon, peeled and deseeded

½ cup coconut meat

1 cup coconut milk

1 cup ice

Instructions

Peel the pineapple, cut the pulp into pieces.

Squeeze fresh lemon juice. To prevent the lemon seeds from entering the cocktail, strain the juice through a fine sieve.

In a blender, combine the pineapple, lemon juice, coconut meat, and coconut milk with ½ cup ice, and blend until thoroughly combined.

While blending, add the remaining ice until the desired consistency is achieved.

Pineapple & Coconut

Coconut meat, banana, and pineapple give this delicious smoothie its unique flavor and texture.

But this combination provides more than just beauty and taste; Vitamin C and phytochemicals like bromelain boost immunity, improve system function, and make this smoothie a versatile winner!

Ingredients

- ½ cup pineapple
- 1 banana, peeled
- 1 cup coconut meat
- 2 cups coconut milk
- ½ cup of ice

Instructions

Peel bananas and pineapple and cut into slices.

In a blender, combine the coconut meat, banana, pineapple, and coconut milk with ½ cup ice and beat until smooth.

While stirring, add the remaining ice until the desired consistency is achieved.

Pineapple & Apple

Who would've thought that the sweet (but tart!) flavors of pineapple could go so well with the light taste of an apple?

Simple, sweet, and whipped up in just minutes, this smoothie provides a delicious treat any time of day.

Ingredients

2 cups pineapple

1 apple, cored

1 cup organic, pure apple juice (not from concentrate)

½ cup ice

Instructions

Peel the pineapple, cut the pulp into pieces.

Peel the apples, core them, and then cut them into slices.

In a blender, combine the pineapple, apple, and apple juice with ½ cup ice, and blend until thoroughly combined.

While blending, add the remaining ice until the desired consistency is achieved.

Heavenly Coconut Delight

Heavenly: The word that best describes the aroma and taste of this deliciously sweet smoothie that combines coconut, banana, vanilla, aromatic spices, sweet maple syrup, and almond aromas.

Ingredients

- 1 cup coconut meat
- 1 banana, peeled
- 1 vanilla pulp
- 1 teaspoon clove, ground
- 1 teaspoon ground ginger
- 1 teaspoon natural organic maple syrup
- 2 cups vanilla almond milk
- 2 cups ice

Instructions

Peel bananas and cut into slices.

In a blender, combine the coconut meat, banana, vanilla bean pulp, cloves, ginger, maple syrup, and almond milk with 1 cup ice and stir until combined.

While stirring, add the remaining ice until the desired consistency is achieved.

Papaya, Orange & Pineapple

This papaya smoothie is one of the tastiest smoothies in my collection. The ingredients also include pineapple and orange. The result is an exotic, multifaceted smoothie flavor. With every sip, this papaya smoothie reveals more and more shades, and with the last sip, you are undoubtedly enjoying yourself.

Papaya flesh can be bright orange, yellowish or pinkish depending on the degree of ripeness. But papaya for smoothies doesn't have to be ripe, with yellow skin and rich reddish-orange flesh. You can use any fruit for a papaya smoothie. You can even add unripe green papaya fruit. The taste will always be great!

Ingredients

1 cup chopped papaya pulp

1 orange

1 cup pineapple chunks (fresh or canned)

1/2 glass of water

A few pieces of ice

Sprig of mint (optional)

Instructions

Wash the papaya, cut in half and remove the seeds, cut the pulp into pieces. Juice the oranges.

You can also use orange pulp, but you must first remove all films so that they do not add bitterness to the drink.

Peel the pineapple, cut the pulp into pieces. You can also use canned pineapple.

Place the fruit in a blender bowl and blend until smooth. Add chilled water and ice cubes, stir again.

For a flavorful smoothie, add a few mint leaves to the fruit and beat well.

The gorgeous papaya smoothie is ready!

Papaya & Banana

Sometimes simplicity is better. It definitely rings true with this delicious blend of sweet papaya, smooth banana, and creamy coconut milk.

In the morning, afternoon, or night, this smoothie remains a deliciously sweet cool treat.

Ingredients

- 2 cups papaya, peeled and pitted
- 1 banana, peeled
- 2 cups coconut milk
- 1 glass of ice

Instructions

Wash the papaya, cut in half and remove the seeds, cut the pulp into pieces.

Peel bananas and cut into slices.

In a blender, combine the papaya, banana, and 1 cup coconut milk with ½ cup ice and beat until smooth.

While stirring, add the remaining coconut milk and ice until the desired consistency is achieved.

Vanilla Papaya

This smoothie combines powerful nutrients and super-health benefits: the disease-fighting beta-carotene in papaya, omega-rich flaxseed, yogurt with probiotics, and the healthy fats and protein in almond milk.

The unmatched taste and strong health benefits make this smoothie unbeatable!

Ingredients

2 cups papaya, peeled and seedless

¼ cup ground flaxseed

½ cup yogurt

1 cup vanilla almond milk

¼ cup of ice

Instructions

Wash the papaya, cut in half and remove the seeds, cut the pulp into pieces.

In a blender, combine the papaya, flaxseed, yogurt, and almond milk with ½ cup ice and beat until smooth.

While stirring, add the remaining ice until the desired consistency is achieved.

Citrus Smoothies

Smoothies are often made from a variety of citrus fruits. The usefulness of citrus fruits is explained by the extraordinary richness of vitamins and minerals. Beta-carotene, folic acid, vitamins of group B, A, B1, B2, B5, B6, C, H, and PP, potassium, calcium, magnesium, zinc, iron, molybdenum, phosphorus, sodium - all these are very useful components.

The rich chemical composition makes these fruits necessary for replenishing the lack of vitamins, enhancing the protective properties of the body, improving the condition of the blood, and the normal functioning of the heart and blood vessels.

Thanks to the anti-microbial and anti-inflammatory properties, as well as the tonic effect, the healing process is accelerated.

Citrus fruits have a fresh, seductive aroma and a juicy texture. Drinks from them invigorate and quench thirst well. Adding orange juice to smoothies makes them healthier and more appetizing. Thick yet juicy orange smoothies have gained popularity for these properties. They are liked by adults and children, they help to quench their thirst, cheer them up, and strengthen the immune system.

Lemon

not only improves drinks and meals but improves the digestion of food thanks to citric acid, which breaks down fats. Lemon perfectly tones the body and is capable of preventing heartburn and nausea. Lemon lowers blood cholesterol and helps the rapid healing of bones in fractures.

Grapefruit

is delicate citrus fruit containing the flavonoid naringenin, which gives it a bitter taste and burns fat. Grapefruit contains essential oils and organic foods that speed up metabolism and improve the digestive process.

Grapefruit is also rich in fiber, which causes the body to flush out toxins. But, despite all this, experts advise using it carefully.

Grapefruit is incompatible with many medications such as blood pressure-lowering drugs, statins, cardiac arrhythmias, etc. Due to grapefruit juice, the effect of drugs can be enhanced or, conversely, suppressed.

Therefore, if you have to take medications for a long time, it makes sense to consult with your doctor if you can combine them with grapefruit.

Orange

in the amount of 1.5 pieces provides the daily requirement of vitamin C. Vitamins A and E have a powerful antioxidant effect and strengthen the immune system. Phosphorus and calcium contained in oranges protect tooth and bone enamel. Potassium ensures the normalization of the nervous and cardiovascular systems. Smoothies made from oranges can be called a "sunshine drink." If you are often in a sad, gloomy, or depressed mood, oranges can help dispel the gloom. They are an ideal food for when you are deprived of sunlight or feeling lonely or empty - oranges will fill you with warmth and light.

Lime

In terms of the content of vitamin C and organic acids, this exotic fruit can compete with lemon. That is why limes are considered a wonderful anti-cold and antibacterial agent. When choosing a lime, remember that fresh fruit should be strong, rich yellowish-green in color. A stale fruit has dry, tough skin with dark spots. Lime spoils very easily, so it is not recommended to purchase it for future use.

Scientists have shown that the smell of citrus fruits has a positive effect on a person's emotional state, improves mood, gives inspiration, increases efficiency, helps to concentrate, relax, and even cope with depression.

Smoothies with grapefruit are included in the diet for those who want to lose weight. This fruit has fat-burning properties, normalizes the functioning of the gastrointestinal tract, and improves immunity.

Peculiarities of making citrus smoothies:

- The film surrounding the orange and grapefruit slices is bitter and difficult to grind. The pulp must be peeled before adding to the blender.

- The smoothie uses both pulp and citrus juice. This only affects the consistency of the drink.

- We recommend taking only fresh and ripe fruits, there is a lot of sugar and additives in canned ones.

- If the recipe contains orange juice, use freshly squeezed juice, not a store-bought one made from concentrates with added sugar and other ingredients that are not very good for your health.

- It is better to squeeze juice from citrus fruits through a special citrus juicer, so that's its yield will be maximized.

Mint Orange

Treat yourself to an interesting mix of mint and orange smoothies.

The name itself refreshes and tones up, and the finished drink turns out to be simply beyond any expectations!

An easy-to-make and extraordinarily aromatic mint and orange smoothie, perfect for breakfast or a quick snack.

Ingredients

1 orange

2 sprigs of mint

1/2 cup natural yogurt

1 teaspoon chopped walnuts (optional)

Blueberries and mint (for topping)

Instructions

Rinse the mint sprigs in cold water. Remove all mint leaves from the twigs. If the mint is young and the stems are not too thick, the whole plant can be used.

If you have a powerful blender and don't mind small chunks in your smoothie, you can add whole kernels. If you want to get the most homogeneous drink, then pre-grind the nuts in a blender or coffee grinder.

Pour the yogurt into a blender bowl. Add orange, mint, and nuts. Whisk at maximum speed until smooth.

Pour the finished mint-orange cocktail into glasses, garnish with blueberries and a sprig of mint.

Orange & Ginger

Cold season prevention can be delicious!

In this difficult period, we advise you to pay attention to a medicinal drink with ginger and orange (tangerine).

Ingredients

2 bananas

2 oranges (or tangerines - 4 pcs.)

1/2 cup almond milk (or yogurt)

1 tsp grated fresh ginger root

Instructions

Grate the ginger on a fine grater.

Remove the peels, white streaks, and seeds from the oranges/tangerines.

Peel the banana, cut it into slices.

Add all the ingredients in this super vitamin smoothie to a blender. Whisk until smooth.

Enjoy!

Spicy Orange

An orange smoothie has many health benefits. Its bright orange color will cheer you up and energize you.

Ginger root, thanks to its sharpness, will help to invigorate in the morning. Try this smoothie and get energized for the whole day!

Ingredients

1 orange

1/2 lemon

1 glass of water

A small piece of ginger root

2-3 sprigs of mint

1 tsp honey - optional

Instructions

Peel the orange and be sure to remove the inner partitions so that the smoothie doesn't taste bitter.

Rinse the mint and pat dry on a paper towel.

Peel and grate the ginger root. Squeeze the juice out of half of the lemon.

Put all ingredients in a blender, beat for 1-2 minutes.

For optimum consistency, add water in portions.
For a sweeter smoothie, add honey.

Orange & Mango

With just a few simple ingredients, this smoothie is easy to make and enjoy.

With unique flavors that work well together, this smoothie gives you a cool and enjoyable experience with every sip!

Ingredients

3 large oranges, peeled and seeded

½ cup peeled mango

1 glass of water

1 glass of ice

Instructions

Peel the orange and be sure to remove the inner partitions so that the smoothie doesn't taste bitter.

Wash, peel, pit, and cut the mangoes.

In a blender, combine the oranges, mangoes, and water with ½ cup ice and beat until smooth.

While stirring, add the remaining ice until the desired consistency is achieved.

Lemon, Coconut & Ginger

If you are looking for unusual shades and piquant tastes, try this wonderful tonic drink, which will perfectly refresh after a long day at work and will pleasantly surprise you with its unique taste.

This coconut-lemon smoothie with the addition of ginger is an unusually refreshing drink with a tart, but very pleasant and original taste.

Ingredients

1 medium coconut

1 lemon

1/2 cup natural yogurt

1 tablespoon honey

1/3 teaspoon grated ginger root

Instructions

Cut a small piece from the ginger root. Peel this piece and grate on a fine grater.

Wash the lemon thoroughly. Cut it into pieces without removing the top layer.

First, drain the milk out of the coconut by poking three holes at the top with a sharp object. Split the nut itself into two parts and cut the pulp out of one of the halves.

Put the lemon slices, chopped ginger, and coconut pulp into a blender bowl, add honey, pour in the yogurt, and add the nut milk. A minute of blender operation will be enough and there is a ready-made smoothie in front of you.

Pour the ginger-lemon smoothie into glasses and enjoy the unusual taste of the drink.

Invigorating Grapefruit & Citrus

Many people like the pleasant bitterness that is characteristic of grapefruit.

This orange, grapefruit, lemon, green tea, banana, and honey smoothie will not only invigorate you but also give you a good mood for the whole day.

This is a delicious and healthy drink for the whole family.

Ingredients

- 1 grapefruit
- 1 orange
- 1 lemon
- 1 banana
- 1 cup of iced green tea
- 2 tablespoons honey

Instructions

Brew your favorite green tea and refrigerate it.

Prepare all the specified fruits - wash and peel. For the orange and grapefruit, carefully remove the thin membranes between the wedges and cut them into slices. Squeeze the juice from the lemon, strain through a fine mesh to remove seeds.

Whisk the orange and grapefruit with lemon juice and green tea in a blender. Add the sliced banana.

Add the specified portion of honey to the puree and beat again. The amount of sweetener can vary based on personal preference. For this reason, try smoothies and add some sweetness if needed.

In hot weather, we recommend adding ice to the composition.

Pour the prepared drink into glasses, decorate with fruit. The smoothie is thin enough that you can easily use a straw.

Grapefruit & Strawberries

Pink grapefruit, pineapple, and strawberries are excellent sources of vitamin C, a powerful natural antioxidant. In addition, this vitamin promotes the absorption of iron, making this smoothie especially beneficial for women.

Ingredients

pulp of a large pink grapefruit

1/2 cups canned or ripe pineapples

1/2 cups fresh or frozen strawberries

1/2 cups yogurt

Instructions

Peel the pineapple, cut the pulp into pieces.

For the grapefruit, carefully remove the thin membranes between the wedges and cut them into slices.

Use a blender to blend large pink grapefruit pulp, pineapple, fresh or frozen strawberries, and plain yogurt.

Pour the smoothie into tall glasses and enjoy!

Grapefruit & Banana

Grapefruit smoothies are a great option to complement your daily menu with a healthy drink.

Grapefruit is recommended as a preventive measure for colds. It is also very useful in the spring to combat vitamin deficiencies.

What's more, grapefruit is known to speed up the body's metabolism, making it an ideal fruit for diet smoothies.

Ingredients

¼ part of grapefruit

1 banana

1 orange

1 tsp honey

Instructions

Prepare all of the specified fruits - wash and peel.
For the orange and grapefruit, carefully remove the thin films between the slices.

First of all, we load the juicy fruits – the orange and grapefruit - into the blender bowl.

After whipping the citrus fruits, a sufficient amount of liquid is formed into which you can throw the chopped banana.

Add the indicated serving of honey to the smooth puree and whisk again at the end. The amount of sweetener can vary based on personal preference. For this reason, try smoothies and add some sweetness if needed.

Pour the prepared drink into glasses, decorate with fruit.

Grapefruit & Pineapple

If you're looking for a smoothie that tastes so delicious that it knocks you off your feet, you've found it!

This surprisingly vibrant blend of brightly tasty pineapple, lemon, and grapefruit are balanced with added vanilla coconut milk.

Ingredients

- 1/2 grapefruit, peeled and seeded
- 1 glass of pineapple
- 1/2 lemon, peeled and pitted
- 1 cup vanilla coconut milk
- 1/3 glass of ice

Instructions

For the grapefruit, carefully remove the thin membranes between the wedges and cut them into slices.

Peel the pineapple, cut the pulp into pieces.

Squeeze the juice from the lemon, strain through a fine mesh to remove seeds.

In a blender, combine the pineapple, lemon juice, grapefruit, and coconut milk with ½ cup ice and beat until smooth.

While stirring, add the remaining ice until the desired consistency is achieved.

Melon & Watermelon Smoothie

In the watermelon season, you can not only eat watermelon but also drink it! Yes, in the form of a refreshing smoothie! Be sure to try it, because it tastes so good!

Watermelon contains vitamins A, E, PP, group B, ascorbic acid. It also contains a powerful antioxidant. This berry is suitable for those who are watching their weight or even trying to lose weight.

Watermelon normalizes the functioning of the digestive system, is useful for diseases of the liver and gallbladder, as well as for constipation. Possessing a diuretic and choleretic trigger, watermelon accelerates the excretion of toxins and salts and improves the functioning of the kidneys and gallbladder. Thanks to its magnesium content, it has a positive effect on the functioning of the nervous system.

Melons, which, in addition, have an unforgettable aroma, have no less bright taste than watermelons. Melons are very healthy. They are rich in fiber, which improves bowel function. Melon also contains Vitamin C, which boosts immunity, promotes collagen production, and protects the skin from sun damage.

Thanks to its high content of folate and other B vitamins, cantaloupe can help promote women's health. However, even such a healthy fruit has contraindications.

Melon is contraindicated for nursing mothers, as it can cause digestive upset in the baby; it is undesirable to use it in case of diabetes mellitus, gastric ulcer, and duodenal ulcer.

In the summertime, you want something cool and refreshing, so when watermelons and melons begin to ripen, they appear in the diet of most people.

One of the options for their use is smoothies. There are many delicious recipes for watermelon and melon smoothies with other ingredients. We offer a selection of the best of them.

Cooking features

Melon smoothies are characterized by a pleasant, delicate taste, they are nutritious and at the same time low in calories. The basis of watermelon drinks is a chilled or frozen fruit without a peel, peeled. To make a melon smoothie, you should also pre-hold it in the refrigerator, remove the seeds and skin, and cut it into cubes.

Since watermelon and melon are quite watery fruits, it is usually not necessary to add water to the smoothie. Natural yogurt, kefir, fruit juice can act as liquid components of a smoothie based on them.

Melon smoothies are quite sweet, so no sweeteners are usually added to them. In contrast, many recipes include sour or sweet and sour ingredients, such as lime, cranberry, or sour apple. This helps balance the sweetness and does not make the finished smoothie too cloying.

Watermelon and melon go well with many fruits like bananas, which gives the smoothie a creamy texture.

In addition, you can add herbs and vegetables such as cabbage or cucumber to melon and watermelon smoothies. This will enrich the drink with fiber and vitamins, but will not degrade the taste of the finished cocktail.

Melon, Mint & Lemon

Looking for something cool and refreshing on a sultry day? Make yourself an invigorating smoothie using lemon, lime, and mint.

These three components are excellent for toning up the body, but the main component of this smoothie is still juicy aromatic melon.

It is the perfect combination where the sugary-sweet melon is complemented by sour lemon and bitter lime, and mint leaves provide a pleasant cooling aftertaste.

Ingredients

1 cup diced melon

¼ part of lime

½ part lemon

1 teaspoon honey (optional)

2 sprigs of mint

a few ice cubes (optional)

Instructions

Remove the pits from the melon and cut the flesh into medium-sized pieces.

Also, remove the seeds from the lemon and lime. The presence of seeds can spoil the taste of the smoothie, making it bitter, so it is best to get rid of them.

Put the prepared ingredients in a blender bowl, add honey. If your melon is very sweet, the honey can be omitted.

Separate the mint leaves from the twigs, rinse, shake off any excess drops and mix with the rest of the ingredients.

Turn the blender on full power and beat until thick and fluffy.

Pour the smoothie into glasses, add ice cubes, garnish with mint and lemon.

Melon & Banana

A wonderful combination of ripe juicy melon and banana is successfully complemented with cinnamon and honey.

And thanks to the yogurt, the drink acquires a creamy consistency.

Ingredients

- 2 cups melon pulp
- 1 banana
- 1 cup natural yogurt
- 1 tbsp. spoon of honey
- A pinch of ground cinnamon
- Mint leaves for decoration

Instructions

Peel the melon and banana, cut into slices, and place in the blender bowl. Beat.

Add yogurt, honey, and cinnamon, stir again.

Pour the smoothie into glasses, garnish with mint leaves and enjoy!

If you want the smoothie to be cold, freeze the banana beforehand (or add a few pieces of ice to the smoothie).

Melon & Kiwi

The pleasant color and fantastically fresh taste of this smoothie are sure to make it one of the family's favorite drinks.

Instead of vanilla soy milk, you can use cow's milk (or yogurt) and add some vanilla.

Ingredients

2 cups melon pulp
1 kiwi
1 apple
1 cup soy vanilla milk
1 tablespoon honey - optional
1 tablespoon lemon juice
1-2 sprigs of mint

Instructions

Pre-chill the milk in the freezer.

Remove the skin from the kiwi and apple, and cut it into slices.

Peel the melon, remove the seeds, and cut it into cubes.

Squeeze the juice out of the lemon.

Rinse the mint and tear off the leaves.

Place the ingredients in a blender and beat for 2-3 minutes.

Pour the smoothie into glasses. Now it's ready!

Melon & Berries

A light, low-calorie blueberry smoothie rich in vitamins and minerals. This drink is good for eyesight, bones, and heart. Since blueberries have a slightly sour taste, it is customary to add something brighter and juicier to them, for example, a fragrant melon.

Melon is also beneficial as it protects the body from stress and stroke. This combination will successfully complement the black currant!

Ingredients

2 cups chopped melon pulp

1/2 cup blueberries

1/2 cup black currant

1/4 cup ice or

1/2 cup oat milk (optional)

Instructions

Grind the melon pulp, wash the blueberries and currants, and grind all the ingredients in a blender.

If you want to make your smoothie even healthier, dilute it with oat milk.

To do this, mix a glass of oatmeal with a liter of boiled water, let the drink brew for 20 minutes, and then beat well and strain.

Place the ingredients in a blender and beat for 2-3 minutes.

Serve the drink in glasses with a sprig of fresh mint!

Watermelon & Grapefruit

Fragrant, healthy, moderately sweet, and with a pleasant bitterness, a watermelon and grapefruit smoothie will perfectly quench not only thirst but also hunger and fill the body with vitamins.

Such a delicious and aromatic drink is prepared in a matter of minutes. | A great start to the day!

Ingredients

2 cups watermelon pulp

1 grapefruit

2 sprigs of fresh mint

Instructions

Separate the pulp of the watermelon from the green rind, cut it into pieces and remove all of the seeds.

Wash the grapefruit, peel, and carefully remove the thin membranes between the slices.

Place the peeled watermelon and grapefruit pulp in a blender bowl and mash.

Rinse the mint well, dry it a little, separate the leaves, and add to a blender. Stir again.

Pour the drink into glasses or cocktail glasses.

Glasses can be garnished with slices of grapefruit or watermelon, as well as fresh mint leaves.

Watermelon & Banana

This delicious smoothie is packed full of hydrating watermelon, smooth banana, and creamy coconut milk that will brighten your day.

Ingredients

- 2 cups watermelon
- 1 banana, peeled
- 1 cup coconut milk
- 1 cup ice

Instructions

Separate the pulp of the watermelon from the green rind, cut it into pieces and remove all of the seeds.

Peel the banana, cut it into slices.

In a blender, combine the watermelon, banana, and coconut milk with ½ cup ice, and blend until thoroughly combined.

While blending, add the remaining ice until the desired consistency is achieved.

Watermelon "Mojito"

This is probably the summeriest smoothie!

Very fresh, tasty, and tender. Indulge yourself and your loved ones with a fragrant and colorful watermelon mojito, which you can easily create in your kitchen in a few minutes.

Ingredients

3 cups chilled (or frozen) watermelon pulp

2-3 sprigs of mint

1/2 lemon or lime

1 cup chilled mineral water

1 tsp honey

Instructions

Wash the watermelon and cut it into pieces. Separate the flesh from the rind, remove the seeds. Place the pulp in the freezer for about an hour.

Wash the lemon, cut them in half, and use a citrus juicer to squeeze out the lemon juice. If you decide to squeeze the juice by hand, you will need more lemons (1 pcs.), And you need to remove the seeds or their fragments from the juice. Determine the sweetness of the drink according to your taste, but remember that lime is very sour!

Before making a smoothie, honey should be melted in a water bath so that it does not lose its beneficial properties.
Mix the melted honey with the lemon juice.

Remove the watermelon pulp from the freezer, put it in the blender bowl, and pour the lemon-honey mixture and a glass of chilled mineral water into it. Rinse the mint stalks, tear off the leaves, and add to the container.
Whisk the ingredients with a blender. Pour the finished smoothie into glasses and garnish with a sprig of mint and a slice of lemon or lime. Enjoy!

Watermelon, Melon & Raspberry

Another perfect combination is watermelon, melon, and raspberry. The sweetness of the watermelon and the freshness of the berries give an indescribable taste.

Raspberries, watermelon pulp, melon - that's all you need for such a cocktail. To set off excessive sweetness, you can add a little lemon or apple juice.

Ingredients

- 1 cup watermelon pulp
- 1 cup melon pulp
- 1 cup raspberries (fresh or frozen)
- 1 glass of water
- 1-2 tsp lemon or lime juice
- 2 sprigs of mint
- Small piece of ginger root (optional)
- A few ice cubes

Instructions

Wash the melon and watermelon, peel, remove all the seeds and cut into pieces. Sort the fresh raspberries and rinse with water. Place these ingredients in a blender bowl and beat until smooth.

Rinse the mint sprigs, tear off the leaves, and add to the blender bowl.

Also add water, lemon, or lime juice, and quite a bit of grated ginger root. Stir again.

The refreshing smoothie is ready!

Watermelon & Strawberries

Watermelon pulp is a real summer salvation at the first signals of dehydration.

And even if you don't pick up these signals, a smoothie will not be superfluous, because few of us drink the 8 necessary glasses of water a day.

Ingredients

2 cups watermelon pulp

1 cup strawberries

1 glass of coconut (almond) milk

2 tbsp lime juice

a handful of ice

Instructions

Wash the watermelon, peel, remove all the seeds and cut into pieces.

Wash the strawberries under running cold water, sort and remove the sepals. If the strawberries are large, cut them in half.

In a blender, combine the watermelon, strawberries, lime juice and coconut milk with ½ cup ice, and blend until thoroughly combined.

While blending, add the remaining ice until the desired consistency is achieved.

Watermelon & Blackcurrant

The sweet and incredibly juicy pulp of watermelon is a great base for making nutritious, yet light and healthy smoothies.

A smoothie made from watermelon with the addition of black currant will only benefit - it will acquire a bright sourness and an incredible berry aroma!

Ingredients

- 2 cups watermelon pulp
- 1/2 cup black currants (fresh or frozen)
- 1 banana
- 1 cup yogurt
- Honey - optional
- 1-2 tsp lemon juice - optional

Instructions

Place the pitted and coarsely chopped watermelon into the bowl of a blender.

Peel the banana, cut it into slices, add to the watermelon.

Rinse the fresh currants well, remove debris and twigs, put them in a blender bowl. Stir.

Add the yogurt, honey, and lemon juice to taste. Stir again.

Pour into glasses and garnish with mint leaves.

INDEX

A

almond milk 108, 152
apple 9, 20, 32, 54, 56, 66, 77, 78, 79, 82, 84, 86, 89, 90, 91, 92, 94, 114, 132, 136, 177, 184, 193
apple juice 84, 86, 144
apples 10, 51, 52, 77, 79, 82, 83, 85, 86, 87, 88, 91, 92, 93, 94, 144
apricot 70, 72, 76
apricots 59, 61, 70, 72, 73, 74, 76

B

banana 9, 18, 20, 22, 27, 28, 32, 36, 38, 42, 46, 47, 48, 50, 56, 63, 67, 68, 70, 72, 76, 84, 89, 90, 100, 114, 118, 125, 126, 127, 128, 129, 130, 134, 136, 138, 141, 142, 145, 146, 149, 150, 160, 167, 168, 172, 181, 182, 189, 190, 198
bananas 10, 21, 64, 68, 83, 121, 136, 138, 142, 146, 150, 177
basil 25, 26, 81, 82, 115, 116, 136
blackcurrant 40
blueberries 17, 45, 46, 48, 158, 185, 186

C

cardamom 87, 88
cherries 17, 101, 102, 103, 104, 106, 108, 110, 112, 114, 115, 116, 118, 120
Cherries 17, 65, 102, 103, 107, 109, 111, 114, 117, 118
cherry 65, 66, 101, 102, 103, 104, 105, 109, 113, 115, 119
chia seeds 120, 129, 130
cinnamon 18, 51, 52, 90, 92, 99, 100, 106, 112, 113, 114, 181, 182
cloves 87, 88, 92, 108, 146
cocoa powder 112
coconut 10, 20, 22, 36, 71, 138, 142, 145, 146, 149, 150, 165, 166, 173, 174, 189, 190, 196
coconut meat 118, 140, 142, 146
Coconut meat 141
coconut milk 10, 22, 36, 138, 139, 140, 142, 149, 150, 173, 174, 189, 190, 196
cranberries 49, 50, 51, 52, 53, 54, 56, 58
currants 16, 36, 37, 38, 40, 42, 186, 198

D

date 112
dates 56

F

flax seeds 120
flaxseed 152
fresh berries 16, 46
fresh ripe blueberries 44
frozen berries 18, 31, 32, 34, 42, 44, 58, 72

G

ginger 18, 29, 30, 54, 56, 57, 58, 87, 88, 92, 95, 96, 100, 108, 119, 120, 146, 159, 160, 162, 165, 166, 194
grapefruit 54, 155, 156, 167, 168, 169, 170, 171, 172, 173, 174, 187, 188
grapes 98
green tea 167, 168

H

honey 18, 20, 28, 32, 36, 40, 42, 44, 46, 50, 51, 52, 53, 54, 64, 72, 74, 88, 90, 94, 96, 98, 100, 106, 110, 112, 116, 120, 127, 128, 129, 130, 131, 132, 162, 166, 167, 168, 172, 180, 181, 182, 192, 198

K

kiwi 9, 122, 125, 127, 128, 129, 130, 131, 184

L

lemon 9, 48, 54, 70, 72, 88, 116, 120, 132, 136, 155, 162, 165, 166, 167, 168, 173, 174, 179, 180, 184, 192, 193, 194, 198
lemon juice 9, 54, 70, 116, 120, 132, 136, 140, 168, 174, 192, 198
lemon zest 48
lemons 93, 94, 192
lime 20, 24, 72, 88, 98, 156, 177, 179, 180, 192, 194, 196

M

mango 18, 86, 121, 124, 126, 133, 134, 136, 137, 138
maple syrup 18, 94, 145, 146
melon 18, 177, 178, 179, 180, 181, 182, 184, 185, 186, 193, 194
milk 12, 26, 28, 33, 40, 42, 46, 48, 58, 63, 71, 72, 76, 96, 100, 106, 120, 146, 166, 183, 184, 186
mineral water 20, 54, 82, 132, 192
mint 20, 36, 38, 40, 42, 46, 48, 64, 76, 98, 113, 114, 132, 148, 157, 158, 162, 179, 180, 182, 184, 186, 188, 192, 194, 198
mint leaves 158

N

nectarine 18, 132
nutmeg 108

O

oat flakes 32
oatmeal 27, 28, 32, 47, 48, 50, 89, 106, 186
orange 54, 70, 74, 100, 133, 134, 147, 148, 156, 157, 158, 159, 161, 162, 164, 167, 168, 172
oranges 10, 70, 121, 134, 148, 155, 160, 164

P

papaya 147, 148, 149, 150, 152
peach 18, 60, 63, 64, 65, 66, 70, 72
peaches 59, 60, 61, 62, 64, 67, 68, 70

R

pear 43, 44, 78, 79, 81, 95, 96, 99, 100, 118
pears 10, 79, 82, 87, 88, 98
pineapple 40, 123, 126, 134, 136, 139, 140, 141, 142, 143, 144, 147, 148, 169, 170, 173, 174

R

raspberries 16, 17, 23, 24, 33, 34, 42, 56, 194
rosemary 100, 131, 132

S

soy milk 40, 71, 183
strawberries 7, 16, 17, 20, 21, 22, 23, 24, 26, 28, 30, 33, 34, 42, 72, 110, 169, 170, 196

V

vanilla 18, 20, 36, 46, 99, 100, 109, 110, 145, 146, 173, 183

W

watermelon 17, 18, 175, 176, 177, 178, 187, 188, 189, 190, 191, 192, 193, 194, 196, 197, 198

Y

yellow kiwis 132
yogurt 7, 21, 22, 23, 24, 26, 28, 30, 33, 34, 36, 37, 38, 39, 42, 44, 47, 48, 50, 52, 62, 63, 64, 65, 66, 74, 90, 106, 109, 110, 112, 114, 116, 118, 120, 152, 158, 166, 170, 177, 181, 182, 183, 198

Printed in Great Britain
by Amazon